Managing Money

By Linda Crotta Brennan

Illustrated by Rowan Barnes-Murphy

The
Child's
World®

Published by The Child's World®
1980 Lookout Drive • Mankato, MN 56003-1705
800-599-READ • www.childsworld.com

Acknowledgments
The Child's World®: Mary Berendes, Publishing Director
The Design Lab: Design and production
Red Line Editorial: Editorial direction

Design elements: Eric Krouse/Dreamstime

ISBN 9781614732419
LCCN 2012932818

Printed in the United States of America
Mankato, MN
July 2012
PA02122

About the Author

Linda Crotta Brennan has a master's degree in early childhood education. She has taught elementary school and worked in a library. Now, she is a full-time writer. She enjoys learning new things and writing about them. She lives with her husband and goofy golden retriever in Rhode Island. She has three grown daughters.

About the Illustrator

Rowan Barnes-Murphy has created images and characters for children's and adults' books. His drawings have appeared in magazines and newspapers all over the world. He's even drawn for greeting cards and board games. He lives and works in Dorset, in southwest England, and spends time in rural France, where he works in an ancient farmhouse.

Money jingled in Tomás's pocket as he walked. He eyed candy bars, comic books, and toys as he wandered the store with Mia.

"What are you going to buy?" he asked.

Mia shook her head. "Just the lemons, sugar, and cups we need for the lemonade stand. I'm not getting anything for myself. I'm going to save my money."

"All of it?" Tomás asked. "For what?"

"A new bike," Mia responded.

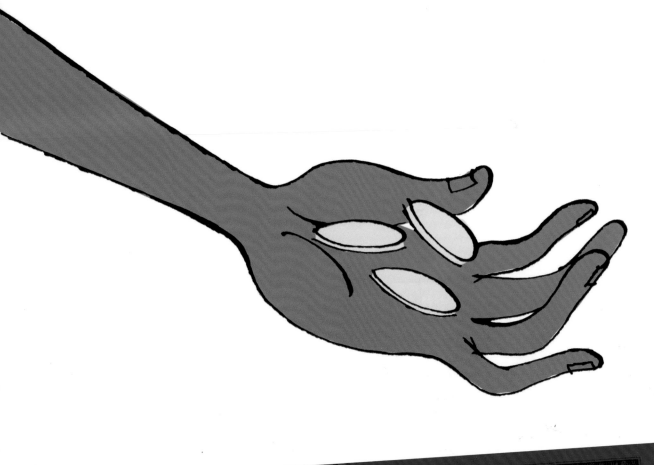

Discover your money habits. Next week, keep track of the money you spend. List what you bought and how much it cost.

Tomás's Uncle Tito and mom were nearby. "It's not good to spend all your money," said Uncle Tito. "But you shouldn't save it all either."

Tomás's mom agreed. "People who are wise about money spend some of it, save some of it, and give some of it to help others. They have a **budget**, a money plan. Not just grown-ups. Kids, too."

Tomás took the change out of his pocket and looked at it. If he spent less on candy and other things, he could save some of his money to buy the video game he's been wanting. "Hey, Mia, when we get back to my house, let's each make a budget," he said.

"That's a good idea," said Mia.

"Uncle Tito, will you help us?" asked Tomás.

"Of course!" he replied.

After putting away their lemonade stand supplies, Tomás and Mia sat down with Uncle Tito. They had paper and pens and were ready to make their budgets.

"How do we start?" Mia asked.

"A budget should start with your **income**," he told them. "If you get a weekly allowance, write it down."

"What about the money I earn mowing Rosita's lawn next door?" asked Tomás.

"List that, too," said Uncle Tito.

"Don't forget what we earn from our lemonade stand," said Tomás.

"That's right!" Mia exclaimed.

"Add up all your income," said Uncle Tito, tapping Tomás's pad. "That's how much money you can plan on each week."

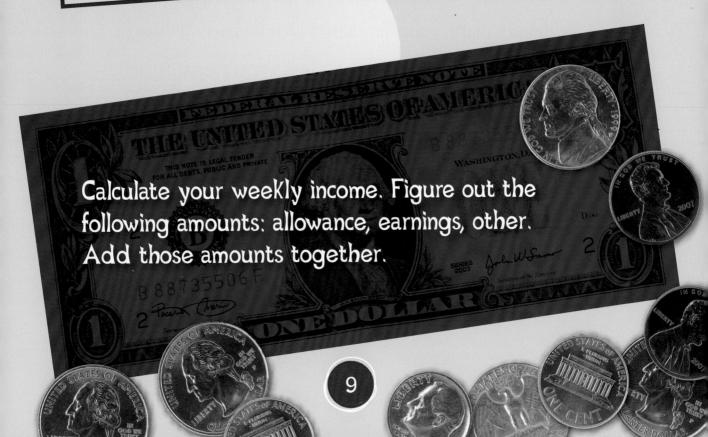

Calculate your weekly income. Figure out the following amounts: allowance, earnings, other. Add those amounts together.

"Spending comes next?" asked Tomás.

"Right." Uncle Tito smiled. "First, figure out your **expenses**. These are the things you need to buy."

"I need to buy chocolate bars and comic books," Tomás declared.

"Those are wants, silly, not needs!" said Mia.

"She's right, Tomás," said Uncle Tito. "Needs are things you must have to live. You need food and clothes, but you don't need candy bars and **expensive** sneakers. Those are things you want."

Mia bounced in her seat. "I know another example," she said. "We need transportation to school, but we don't need to take a taxi or a limousine."

"Good one!" said Uncle Tito.

"So, what needs do I pay for?" asked Mia. "I can't think of any."

"That's because your family pays for your needs. They usually buy the groceries and pay for your house."

"And things like water and electricity, right?" Tomás added.

"Exactly," Uncle Tito replied.

"Wait!" Mia shouted. "I thought of a need. The lemonade stand! Tomás and I bought supplies for it today."

"You're right, Mia. Add that to your list of weekly needs," said Uncle Tito. "Add them up. Next, subtract the needs total from your income. The amount you have left is extra each week."

Tomás and Mia showed Uncle Tito their totals. Both figured out that they had more income than expenses.

"That's great, kids," said Uncle Tito. "How will you use your extra money? Your choices will depend on your **goals**."

"I'd like to see that new animated movie," said Mia.

"That's a short-term goal," said Uncle Tito. "It's something you plan to pay for soon, in the next few weeks."

"There's a video game I want, but it's expensive," said Tomás.

"Then you'll need to save for a while," Uncle Tito explained. "That's a long-term goal."

Think of things you'd like to have or do. Make a list of your short-term goals and long-term goals.

"Now comes the fun part," Uncle Tito said. "Figure out how you're going to reach your goals. How much will you spend now? How much will you save for your goals?"

Tomás scratched his head. "A candy bar costs $1. If I buy three candy bars and eat half each day, that would cost me $3 each week. I would have $6 left over to save for that video game."

Mia jumped up. "But at Saverama, you can buy three candy bars for $2. If you do that, Tomás, you'll have $7 left to save toward your video game."

"That's a great idea. Thanks!" said Tomás.

Spend smart. Look for bargains. If you pay less for one thing, you'll have more money to spend on something else.

"Wait," said Mia. "I think we're forgetting something. Your mom mentioned giving money to help others. My family **donates** money."

"Giving is important," said Uncle Tito.

Tomás nodded. "Miss Singh talked to us in class about an earthquake. All those people lost their homes and belongings."

"My Aunt Donna is a nurse," said Mia. "She told me some children don't have enough food to eat. And they can't afford medicine when they're sick."

"Don't forget the animals," said Tomás. "I want to help save **endangered species**."

"And take care of abandoned pets, like the ones at the animal shelter," added Mia.

"It's a great idea to include giving in your budget," said Uncle Tito. "You've noted some really good ideas for donating some of your money."

"What's next?" asked Tomás.

"Well," said Uncle Tito, "the next step is to put your plans into action."

"How do we do that?" asked Tomás.

"Some kids use three jars," replied Uncle Tito. "They label one 'Spend,' one 'Save,' and the third 'Give.' They put a set amount of money in each jar every week."

"Is it OK to use envelopes instead?" asked Mia.

"Sure," Uncle Tito answered. "The important thing is to stick to your budget."

"I know what I'm going to do with my extra money this week," said Mia. "I'll put $2 in a spend envelope, $4 in a save envelope, and $1 in a give envelope. That will leave $5 for my bank account."

"I'm going to use jars instead of envelopes," added Tomás. "I'm going to divide my money between them."

"You two are money wise!" said Uncle Tito.

Mia and Tomás slapped hands as they chanted, "We're budget pros!"

Glossary

budget (BUHJ-it): This is a money plan that shows money earned and spent. Tomás and Mia created budgets for themselves.

donate (DOH-nate): To give money or goods to a charity is to donate. Tomás and Mia decided to donate part of their extra money.

endangered species (en-DAYN-jurd SPEE-sheez): This is a plant or animal that is at risk for no longer existing, likely because of something humans have done. Tomás wants to donate money to help endangered species.

expense (ik-SPENS): An expense is the cost of or the price paid for something. As part of making a budget, Tomás and Mia listed their expenses.

expensive (ik-SPENS-iv): To cost a lot of money is to be expensive. The video game Tomás wants to buy is expensive.

goal (gohl): Something you want to do is a goal. Tomás has a long-term goal of buying an expensive video game.

income (IN-kuhm): Income is money that a person earns or is given. As part of making a budget, Tomás and Mia listed their income.

Books

Giesecke, Ernestine. *Dollars & Sense: Managing Your Money*. Chicago: Heinemann Library, 2002.

Harman, Hollis Page. *Money Sense for Kids!* 2nd ed. Hauppauge, NY: Barron's, 2005.

McCrary, J. *My Money and Me: Managing Money & Credit*. Mechanicsburg, PA: Westcom, 2010.

Web Sites

Visit our Web site for links about managing money:
childsworld.com/links

Note to Parents, Teachers, and Librarians: We routinely verify our Web links to make sure they are safe and active sites. So encourage your readers to check them out!

Index